MW00881875

GET YOUR CAREER LIFE IN ORDER

Written by
Tana M. Session
Foreword by
Mandy Aragones

Title ID: 1540863158
ISBN-13: 978-1540863157

TABLE OF CONTENTS

DEDICATION

I dedicate this book to all of the career seekers and job hunters who are looking to make a successful transition in today's job market. This guidebook is for you!

FOREWORD

Landing your dream career is tough. And if you're pursuing a promotion, raise or completely new vocation, things could be harder. You're concerned – or lost – or even a little anxious.

Yes, job seekers often misjudge the difficulty of the planning, application and interviewing process. And advancing beyond getting hired also takes know-how. The methods are easy to learn. Just heed the sage advice in Tana M. Session's Get Your Career Life in Order, distilled from her many years in the game.

Tana's a human resources expert and certified life coach. Get Your Career Life in Order is a plainspoken, step-by-step guide for strivers of all shades and stripes, providing easy-to-follow strategies and approaches for successfully navigating the employment market, finding a professional path and improving the quality of one's life. It's all about personal growth, living bold and blooming. She offers special consideration to minorities and seniors, and includes a long list of handy resources (providing an 11 step guide for the five generations competing in the market place on how to "grow their career") and even her email address. This does not surprise me one bit.

Tana is an HR rock star: intelligent, imaginative and inspiring. A Brooklyn, New York native, she grew up in one of America's impoverished inner cities. She climbed the corporate ladder without sacrificing a single ounce of her identity and authenticity. She is unstoppable!

—

5

Tana is also my sister-friend. We connected decades ago, and I have been in awe of her dedication to excellence and advancement ever since. Working in executive positions in human resources for several New York and California companies, she preaches only what she has faithfully practiced. Beyond her many business triumphs, she's also an outstanding mother and exceptional wife.

The willingness with which she shares her knowledge, to help others reach their goals, is something to admire. Tana's gifted my husband and me many pearls of wisdom through the years, which have helped boost our personal and business goals. She influenced me, for example, to share the good things happening in my career, to own my successes and to grow towards the blessings that were designed for me.

Tana pours every bit of her soulful expertise and "get it done" passion into Get Your Career Life in Order. I have a strong conviction that you will find her words positively impactful. From nurturing your personal network and getting noticed, to the art of the interview and understanding what inspires employers most, she brings a lifetime's experience of sustaining companies and shaping careers into original, practical advice. Get Your Career Life in Order is a dynamic and fun read, with no area left uncovered.

~ Mandy Aragones

INTRODUCTION

This book is designed to guide those who are seeking to grow their careers. Whether you are looking to transition to a new job or career, or a transfer or promotion within your current organization, you will gain insight into what it will take to move toward successfully accomplishing that professional goal.

I have gathered a wealth of knowledge through 20-plus years as a Human Resources professional. Each chapter is filled with useful tips that have been documented in an easy to follow, guidebook. Various examples and useful resources are also provided to help reinforce the information provided throughout the book.

Feel free to send me an email and let me know if you found this book helpful. My contact information is provided in the back of this book.

Let's get started and GOOD LUCK on your journey!!

TIP 1 – So You Want a New Job...Now What?

Over the years, I have coached organizations, employees, family members, friends, and co-workers on methods to help change or grow their career. This book is a consolidation of the advice I have shared that has led to job and career success. Whether you are pursuing a new job or career, or seeking a promotion or transfer at your current employer, you should incorporate the same easy-to-follow tips outlined in this guidebook. Let's begin with an initial self-assessment exercise.

Discover Your "WHY"

Before starting out on a job search, it is imperative to know your "WHY":

- WHY now?
- WHY this particular position/promotion?
- WHY this particular company?
- WHY this particular career path?

Taking time to pause and answer each of these questions will help you narrow your focus and target your job search, whether you are considering an internal or external career move. Your responses to this exercise will help you stay focused and spend your energy in the right areas. Looking for a new job can feel like a full-time job, so why not spend that time on the right companies and positions for you?

Know What You Do and Don't Want

Just as important as knowing your "WHY" is knowing what you DO and DON'T want from your next opportunity. Again, the same rules apply, whether the career move is an internal or an external position. Make your list and compare the Pros and Cons. Consider what type of company culture you will excel in and what type of management style works best for you.

Example:

What I DO Want	What I DON'T Want
Casual dress code	Formal/Business Casual dress code
Free drinks and food	Lack of teamwork
Fast-paced and nimble	Competitiveness
Autonomy	Office Politics
Great team collaboration	Lack of diversity
A trusting and trustworthy manager	Micro-Manager
Fair salary and benefits	Unfair compensation practices
Work that matters	Boring work
Work/Life Balance	Long Hours/On-Call

You can see from the example above how it can be very helpful to consider all of the key factors throughout this exercise (i.e., company culture, management style and, of course, compensation). Managing your expectations around what you do and don't want is a necessary exercise throughout career management. This exercise, along with "knowing your why", will help you target your search and remain focused, as well as save you time during your job search. When presented with opportunities by headhunters, mentors or others in you network, you will also know when an opportunity is not a good fit for you. It is completely fine to say "thanks, but no thanks" when it is not the right opportunity for you. You will not lose out on future opportunities by declining one that is not a good fit based on your assessment exercise. Rather, you will ensure that you are available for the right opportunity and perform at your best, thereby protecting your personal brand.

When you think about what you do and don't want, you should take time to consider everything from soup to nuts. Of course it is important to think about total rewards (i.e., salary, benefits and paid time off), but you should also think about career growth and opportunity. Always consider if this position is going to lead you to where you want to be in the long term or if it is just a *job*.

There are distinct differences between a **CAREER** and a **JOB**:

- *JOB*: "a paid position of regular employment" (*google.com*)
- *CAREER*: "an occupation undertaken for a significant period of a person's life and with opportunities for progress" (*google.com*)

A **job** is something that you do from 9 am to 5 pm: you leave all responsibilities at the door when you walk out at the end of the day, and you pick them back up when you return in the morning. You know you are working in a **career** when you really pour yourself into and truly invest in the work that you are doing each day. For example, you are actively completing ongoing educational courses and you are really investing your time, energy and mental capacity into growing professionally within that particular field or industry.

Think about why you are considering making a career move now. Also, when you want to make the move, are you making the move because it aligns with a targeted career goal, or are you making the move because you just need a job, you need to make more money or you need better benefits? Or are you making the move because you were laid off in your current position and you are just looking to make sure that you do not have a gap in employment and compensation?

Making those decisions, starting a list for yourself of knowing your "why", and then drilling down even deeper to understand what you do and don't want from your next opportunity is very important to do before you actually begin applying and interviewing. These initial exercises will help you establish solid targets and set the basic foundation for your "why" as well as what you **DO** and **DON'T** want.

You should also consider partnering with a certified Career Coach when you decide to seek a new job, transfer or promotion. The role of the Career Coach is to:

- Partner with you during your self-assessment exercise
- Help you navigate the current job market for your preferred industry
- Provide candid feedback on your resume and cover letter
- Help you prepare for interviews
- Provide guidance on successful networking
- Provide various tools and resources to reinforce career management guidance (i.e., books, websites and articles)

WORKSHEET

WHY now?	
WHY this particular position/promotion?	
WHY this particular company?	
WHY this particular career path?	

What I DO Want	What I DON'T Want

TIP 2 – The Best Ways to Job-Hunt

The job market has experienced a significant shift since the 2008 crash. Employers are now much more selective when hiring new talent, resulting in up to 90+ days to bring in a new hire. Companies have to scan through hundreds, if not thousands, of resumes to find the best fit for their organization. Over the years, most recruiters have incorporated the use of Applicant Tracking Systems (ATS) to help manage the sheer volume of resumes they receive for each job posting. Candidates need to understand how the standard ATS operates to help ensure their resume rises to the top of the pile. Let's take a look at the best ways to job-hunt in the current job market.

The most important process of job-hunting is to be *targeted* in your job search. This includes researching various industries and companies to ensure they fit within the results of your self-assessment exercises from **TIP 1**. Use resources such as Google©, Glassdoor©, LinkedIn©, as well as the annual Fortune 100 Best Companies to Work For© and Great Place to Work©.

A good job application tracker is also recommended. This will enable you to keep track of the various companies and positions you applied for, as well as any follow-up interviews and contact names. Some candidates opt to use an Excel© spreadsheet. However, JibberJobber© is a great online tracker that allows candidates to upload the resume and other documents submitted with each application. This is quite useful since your resumes should be customized for each position you apply for throughout the job-hunting process.

Online Applications

Job boards and company websites can serve as useful tools in job-hunting. There are several job boards that aggregate multiple company job postings in one central location. These resources can be a timesaver for the job-hunter, eliminating the need to visit multiple company career websites. Additionally, you can set up alerts based on the types of jobs or companies you have on your targeted list that you established in your **TIP 1** self-assessment exercise.

The caveat with job boards and company websites is that you are one of many who have applied for the position. So, how do you gain the attention of the recruiter or hiring manager? How do you ensure that your application and resume do not end up in a "black hole"? Well, this is truly the chance you take when applying electronically for positions. Unless your resume has the necessary verbiage to help it rank higher in the algorithm built into the system, your application will remain dormant after you receive the perfunctory "thank you for applying" auto-response email built into the ATS by the recruiting professionals.

Be certain to read *TIP 3 – Is Your Resume Ready?* for more tips on how to ensure your resume rises to the top of automated ranking systems.

Referrals

Hiring managers and recruiters tend to pay attention to resumes they receive from current employees faster than resumes submitted through the ATS. People tend to want to work with people they know and like, which means they tend to refer people who fall into those categories. Current employees have a great sense of the types of personalities and skill sets that will do well at their company. Referrals tend to rank higher as it relates to gaining traction in the application process.

If you want to get your resume presented to a hiring manager or recruiter as a true referral, be certain to consider who you personally know at your targeted companies. These should be individuals who can really speak to your corporate "fit", work ethic, experience and reliability, and represent you favorably to the recruiter or hiring manager at their company. Referrals can come through friends or family, and still remain within the company's **nepotism** policy and guidelines. Generally, as long as the person who referred you is not your immediate manager, and as long as you and the person who referred you do not report to the same manager, then your referral will be considered by the recruiter and hiring manager.

- *NEPOTISM*: "the practice among those with power or influence of favoring relatives or friends, especially by giving them jobs" (*google.com*).

Direct Contact

Informational interviews and directly reaching out to hiring managers is another way to get noticed. Hiring managers may be open to conducting 15 – 30 minute informational interviews where candidates can learn more about the company, specific projects or about the career path of the hiring manager. The goal of the informational interview is to learn as much as you can, and briefly share how your experience and specific skills may serve as a benefit in the near or long-term for that manager and his team. These interviews can be conducted within your own organization or with companies you have on your target list. It may take multiple requests to get on the calendar of these decision-makers, but once you are successful, make the most of your time with him/her and leave a positive impression. As with any interview, come prepared with questions and take lots of notes. Send a follow-up thank you note (written or email), and occasionally check in with the manager to see how projects are progressing. You will eventually be able to add this manager to your "network".

Networking

Networking is a term that is used quite loosely. Your network must be continually refined, refreshed, finessed and kept "warm", especially when you are not actively looking for a new job. Networking generally involves professional organizations, LinkedIn© connections, and various local networking events. Networking takes work and a fair amount of effort. As the saying goes, *"Your network is your net worth"*. This means that your network will help lead you to new opportunities that can and will increase your income, whether employed with a company or self-employed.

Do not underestimate the importance of a good and active network. The earlier you can develop and establish connections at targeted companies or positions, the better it will serve you when you need to tap into your network. When attending industry-specific events, be certain to exchange business cards with attendees, and follow up with them within one to three (1 – 3) days following your initial introduction. Following up can come in the form of a quick email, or by asking to add them to your LinkedIn© network. Invite the contact to connect over coffee or lunch, or a quick call. Fortunately, LinkedIn© also provides an easily manageable method to stay connected by providing daily alerts about people in your network (i.e., new position, birthday and work anniversary). This is an effortless way to acknowledge the career success of your connections and recognizing them in a timely manner. You will get as much out of your network as you put into your network. Engaging with your network can help expedite and get your resume in front of the right people at your targeted companies. The best piece of advice regarding networking is to consistently and constantly keep in touch with your connections, and give as much as you hope to gain from your network. For example, volunteering, sharing relevant articles and offering to help out on special projects are all great ways to "give back" to professionals in your network. Successful networking is truly a two-way street.

*"Look to **feed** before you **eat!**" – anonymous*

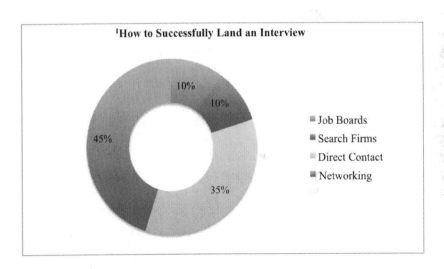

Be Mindful of Peak Interview and Hiring Times

As with any business practice, there are peaks and valleys for interviewing and hiring each year for organizations, which are oftentimes linked to the start and end of the fiscal year and annual budget allocation. Companies can take 45 to 60 days to fill most positions, and 90+ days for more senior-level positions. Candidates can expect to see an increase in new positions and active hiring during the first quarter of each year, which is usually when most departments receive their approved annual headcount and budgets. The next wave of hiring generally takes place in May and June, primarily for college graduates. There is significant slowdown during July and August, which are the summer vacation months, so most hiring managers are not readily available for interviews. Finally, during the holiday months, November through January, is another slow period. Candidates may receive quicker initial responses to applications from recruiters during this time period. However, interviews with hiring managers may not get scheduled until after the holiday season due to vacation schedules. Do not discount the advantage of reaching out to hiring managers or decision makers directly during the holiday months, as many of them are home with family and may welcome the interruption of engaging with a solid candidate for one of their open positions. Professional organizations tend to host holiday parties, which can be another great opportunity to network and let people know you are looking for new opportunities.

Companies that pay out bonuses have historically experienced an uptick in resignations post-bonus season, which varies based on the industry (i.e., financial services generally pay bonuses in March/April). Candidates can sometimes see increases in open positions during this time of year as well. Once you are targeted towards a specific industry, you should track their recruiting ebbs and flows through the job postings and how long those postings remain open on the company's website. This is the best way to track the recruiting movement and plan your job-seeking strategy accordingly.

TIP 3 - Is Your Resume Ready?

The job market has changed over the past decade. Since the market crash of 2008, companies have become more strategic in how they recruit for talent. We have also experienced a renewed *War for Talent*. Candidates are more knowledgeable now and, depending on the industry, understand that they have choices and do not have to settle for the first offer they receive from a potential employer.

However, how candidates present themselves to the market has significantly changed as well. What talent acquisition professionals look for when screening resumes has changed, and candidates need to know what those changes are to ensure their resume rises to the top of the pile.

Have you ever wondered what it really takes to get your resume noticed? Depending on the position, if you do not have someone on the inside of an organization that can walk your resume into the hiring manager's office, it can be quite frustrating and difficult. Recruiters and hiring managers are screening hundreds, if not thousands of resumes each week. What will it take in today's market to get a phone screen or interview for your dream job?

I strongly suggest you use your network to help in your job search. The saying that "your network is your net worth" has never been more true than today. If you do not have an active network, get out there and start establishing one. Now yes, you can apply directly on a company's website or other online job board, but what will truly make you stand out? Your resume is your brand and you are the product. You want your brand to represent you in the best possible way. First impressions last, and the resume is the first tool you have available to represent you to recruiters and hiring managers. By utilizing each of these resume pointers and updating your resume accordingly, you will have an increased chance of having your resume rise to the top of the pile for recruiters and hiring managers.

[2]Top 10 Resume Fonts (*sizes 10 – 14 acceptable*)

Calibri (*email default*)
Times New Roman (*corporate*)
Arial (Geneva) (*marketing*)
Verdana (*clean/modern*)
Cambria (*recruiter-friendly*)
Garamond (*artistic types*)
Book Antiqua (*arts/humanities*)
Trebuchet MS (*creative types*)
Arial Narrow (*modern*)
Didot (*artistic*)

Resume Pointer #1

Your resume should include your best contact information. Be certain to use the phone number and/or email address that you have access to most often throughout the day. Recruiters are contacting several people in response to one job posting, and will rarely call you back or email you a second time. The saying that "first impressions last" is certainly true in this instance. A good best practice is to respond to resume inquiries within 24 hours, if not sooner. In today's job market, things are moving so fast, the expectation is that candidates are responsive and will get back to recruiters within the same day.

With regard to your personal contact information on your resume, in today's age of identity theft, it is commonplace to only list your city and state to ensure that your street address remains confidential until absolutely required by the potential employer. Your full address and other personal information are collected on the company's application, and it is their responsibility to protect your personal data. Resumes are usually not subject to that same level of personal data protection.

Resume Pointer #2

For experienced candidates, a declarative header with a clear and concise title and summary of your expertise should be at the top of your resume. This is your opportunity to briefly tell the recruiter or hiring manager how your skills can help solve their problems. Your summary is a powerful branding tool that helps to demonstrate that you are the right person for the job. Consider a job posting as a company's cry for help. Your resume summary should be relevant to the requirements of the job description and strong enough to grab the attention of the person screening resumes. Key words that will help your resume appear in higher rankings in applicant tracking systems and Boolean searches are important throughout the resume, but be certain to include them in your summary as well. This is where you get to make your initial "sell" and really pitch your expertise and abilities, but this section should not be a repeat of information provided later in your resume. Be brief (2 – 4 sentences maximum or bullet points), but strong and succinct. This summary can also serve as an elevator pitch and a way to introduce yourself when in networking or other professional and social circles. The summary section is also where you should highlight transferrable skills. These are the skills that transfer with you to every new job, and are the core foundation of your overall skill set (i.e., project management, teamwork, leadership or presentation skills). Be certain to highlight your expertise and any major results you have accomplished in previous roles. You may also opt to highlight (**bold font**) key phrases linked to the job description to draw the eye of the reviewer. Studies show that recruiters will review your resume for 6 seconds. Make every second count!

Example:

HUMAN CAPITAL LEADER

Business-savvy, results driven and team-oriented leader with solid credentials, combined with expertise in developing, leading and maximizing performance of individuals and diverse teams. Strong leader in driving change and championing company values, vision and expectations. A strategic business partner and facilitator for innovative initiatives to attract key talent required to address today's business challenges of attaining revenue growth, client satisfaction and retaining top talent.

For those with less experience, this space can be used for your resume objective statement. Your objective statement is an opportunity to express what you would like to accomplish by working for that particular organization in that new role. This statement should remain fluid, and will need to be updated based on the type of position and company to which you are submitting your resume each time.

Resume Pointer #3

The next key part of the resume is your experience. This is where you get to list in chronological order, including month and year(s) of employment, the experience you have to date, beginning with your most recent experience. This should include the employer's name, city and state, month and year(s) of employment, job title(s) and key accomplishments. Depending on your level of experience you may or may not need to include your actual job duties. Recruiters can generally tell by the job title what the standard duties are for the positions. The more senior the job title and responsibilities, the more important it is to represent your <u>key accomplishments</u> versus a listing of your job duties. Listing job duties may be more relevant for those who are just starting out their careers, or in more junior roles.

It is very important to include the month and year of employment. Some candidates will only put the year(s) of employment, but this often raises a red flag with recruiters and hiring managers. By only listing the years, it is difficult to determine the true length of employment. For instance, you may list a position as 2014 – 2015, but only started at the company in November 2014. Therefore, the initial perception is that you were employed with the company for at least one full year, when in fact you may have only been employed for a few months (i.e., November 2014 – February 2015). This is a tactic that some candidates use to minimize showing short periods of employment or gaps in employment, but a good recruiter will certainly pick up on this and consider it deceptive. If there are gaps in your employment, represent them appropriately on your resume, and come to the interview prepared to discuss how you filled that time (i.e., volunteering, continuing education courses, or temporary assignments). Again, first impressions last, so being honest and transparent up front will save you embarrassment, and ultimately elimination, at some point during the interview process.

This is also another section where you want to be certain to include action verbs, use the proper tense (past or present) and have key words based on the job description that will ensure your resume shows up in Boolean search results. Remember, this is your first opportunity to demonstrate how you can help solve the hiring manager's problem. Also, eliminate acronyms or jargon specific to your current or previous employers. Sometimes more is better, so spelling out acronyms so that the recruiter and hiring manager can truly understand what you are representing is best practice.

Do the research and, where possible, use the prospective employer's language when describing your job duties or key accomplishments. Depending on the types of positions you are applying for, you may need to have more than one resume. This generally means that you will have a customized resume for each position for which you are applying. Although time-consuming, this is best practice and will represent to the recruiter and hiring manager that you have a strong sense of what is required for the position. Using the company's key words and phrases will also help your resume rank higher in the ATS, ensuring a higher likelihood of having your resume reviewed earlier in the screening process.

For example, you may be applying for a position in a field you have minimal experience in, but may have done some volunteer work in that particular field or industry. You will want to have a different "specialty" resume for those positions where you can clearly demonstrate how your volunteer experience is relevant and transferable, and can serve you in successfully transitioning to this new career field.

If you have gaps in your employment due to taking time off to take care of children or other personal matters, I recommend you acknowledge that during the initial interview process, and not directly on your resume or cover letter. This is an acceptable practice, but should be discussed one-on-one with the recruiter or hiring manager once you are being considered as a viable candidate for the position.

Resume Pointer #4

The next section of your resume should include your education, listed in chronological order (i.e., graduate degree then undergraduate degree). If you are an experienced professional, it is not necessary to include your GPA, academic awards or your high school information. For those candidates who are new college graduates, you may want to include your GPA, academic awards, and any special student organizations you belonged to in college, including fraternities or sororities. Be certain to include the year of completion, type of degree and major.

Example:

University of Pennsylvania
Bachelor Degree - Business Administration   2012

If you are a candidate who did not complete a college degree, you should include any college courses or relevant certification courses you have completed throughout your career. This is an opportunity for you to demonstrate how you have developed yourself over the years, outside of completing a standard college degree. Candidates should never include the year of their high school graduation. For experienced candidates, elimination of both high school and graduation date is highly recommended. Eliminating this information on your resume will help ensure that recruiters and hiring managers cannot estimate your age, which can result in age discrimination and unconscious bias.

Resume Pointer #5

Some candidates may find that listing special skills can be useful in demonstrating additional transferrable experience you have that is relevant to the job for which you are applying. This section can include relevant computer skills, specialized training/certifications, and professional or industry organizations you have been an active member of throughout your career.

Resume Pointer #6

Please...Please...Please...Double-check your resume for spelling, grammatical errors and verb tense! This is the "kiss of death" for candidates with most recruiters. The thought is that if you cannot spend enough time checking your resume for errors, then you will demonstrate the same lack of attention to detail in your new role. Check for misspelled names and action verbs; incorrect verb tenses; misused homophones (i.e., your/you're, there/their); and inconsistent spellings or use of the same terms (i.e., 09/06, Sept. 2006 and September 2006).

BONUS Resume Pointers

When possible, experienced candidates should make every effort to keep their resumes under three (3) pages. Remember, start off with a strong summary and highlight key accomplishments for each of your positions.

For those who are new to the job market, a one-page resume should be sufficient to present your experience and education. The use of bullet points under the job titles to highlight your job duties will help fill the page to ensure it is at least one full page in length.

Candidates who work as consultants in the IT industry, or other consultant-based roles, may have resumes that are 3+ pages long. However, it is also important to focus on key projects and/or accomplishments that are truly relevant to the position you are currently applying for to ensure the relevance of what you are presenting.

If you have been in your position or employed with the same employer for a long period of time (i.e., over 10 years), then consider a **Functional** resume format versus the standard **Chronological** resume format. The Functional format is designed to emphasize your core transferrable skills and career achievements under each of those skills. It is quite easy to locate samples of both of these types of resumes on the internet. Just conduct an internet search for chronological or functional resume samples based on the title of the position. Regardless of the resume format, do not forget to include key words in your new resume based on the specific job description you are actively pursuing.

Another useful resume pointer is to be certain to keep your LinkedIn© profile updated to match your resume. Although your LinkedIn© profile does not have to be a full replica of the information provided on your resume, the employers, job titles and dates should match. Depending on your industry and job level, LinkedIn© is often the first resource recruiters and hiring managers will use to find out about a candidate, or locate "passive candidates" (those not actively seeking new opportunities). This is particularly true for difficult-to-fill positions or those positions where the right candidates have not been identified through the company's ATS.

Resume Pointer for Professionals of Color

Unconscious bias does exist…and we ALL suffer from it! This particular bias is not necessarily linked to ethnicity or gender, but they are a couple of the most common areas of unconscious bias. As the head of Human Resources for several companies, and one who has managed recruiting for several types of companies over the years, I have witnessed Professionals of Color alter their name on their resume, if it was deemed more mainstream, to help them secure an interview. This is definitely a personal choice, but one I would recommend considering depending on the type of company you are interested in working for.

Example #1:

Full Legal Name = Born Justice Davis
Updated Resume Name = B.J. Davis
This candidate was only being contacted for retail and restaurant positions, even though he held a Bachelor's degree in Business Administration. Once he updated the name on his resume and applied for corporate jobs again, he received phone and in-person interviews and landed a position with a well-known bank, where he has been promoted over the years and is now a Manager. He has since asked to be called "B.J." at work and in all professional settings.

Example #2:

Full Legal Name = Jose C. Williams
Updated Resume Name = Joe C. Williams
This candidate did not receive any requests for interviews after applying multiple times for retail positions. Once he changed the name on his resume, he was contacted by recruiters and ultimately landed the job of his dreams. Once hired, he let the payroll department know what his full name was, but asked to be called "Joe" at work.

Example #3:

Full Legal Name = Hortense Chin
This candidate was called in for several interviews throughout her career because the recruiter and/or hiring manager automatically assumed she was Asian-American based on her name. She is actually African-American, and is certain she was declined positions because she was not what the recruiter/hiring manager expected to see when she walked through their door.

You should always seek out companies where you can be your true, authentic self at work, whatever that means to you. If you are not true to yourself, it is possible that you may fail to achieve your highest level of potential, productivity and success. Standing in your truth is a personal assessment, and one that you will truly recognize when it happens, even if you are addressed by a different name at work while building your credentials, experience and income.

[3]Additional Important Resume Details

- Use legible, clean fonts. Recommend Arial or Calibri
- Size: 11 or 12 PT
- Use selective **BOLDING** for key words and quantifiable metrics
- Margins: Recommend .6" to .75"
- White space is your friend
- Proofread!
- Grammar: Do the tenses match?
- Add hyperlinks where relevant (e.g., personal LinkedIn© URL)

[4]Key Words to Use in Resumes and Cover Letters

Solved	Innovative	Promoted	Trained
Built	Improved	Introduced	Adapted
Assessed	Directed	Initiated	Persuaded
Organized	Managed	Projected	Lead/Led
Oversaw	Strengthened	Planned	Proactive

<u>Resume Template</u>

Title and Summary:	
Expertise:	
Results:	
Chronological Experience:	
Key Accomplishments per Position:	

Education:	
Specialized Skills/Training:	

TIP 4 - Sharpen Your Interview Skills

The best piece of advice I have for you regarding interviewing is to **BE PREPARED**. Do your research on the company and ensure you understand how they make their money and who their competitors or peer companies are in their specific industry. Check out websites such as Glassdoor©, Indeed© and Career Bliss©, which allows current and former employees to post comments about their experience working for that particular company, inclusive of salaries, company culture and workplace experiences. Since the company cannot manipulate the content on these websites, they serve as a great resource for potential candidates.

It is also useful to research the interviewer using LinkedIn© and Google© to learn more about their role with the organization and their specific career path. Perhaps you both worked for the same employer at one time, or attended the same college. This information can help serve as a good icebreaker and help you both relax during the interview process.

Be certain to ask targeted questions throughout your interview(s), and take notes that you can reference during follow-up interviews. Keep in mind that your resume is only the first step in the interview process. Candidates should remain mindful of how they present themselves throughout the hiring process, including phone interviews, in-person interviews and all follow-up communications.

It is extremely important to always dress appropriately for the interview based on the culture of the organization. Arrive at least 15 – 20 minutes early for the interview, but no earlier, as it can be disruptive in the interviewer's day to have a candidate waiting for 30 minutes or more. Ask for directions and, if applicable, parking instructions in advance to ensure you know where you are going. This will help to reduce your anxiety and ensure a timely arrival with minimal issues before your interview begins. Finally, be nice to everyone you meet: the receptionist, security guards, and other employees. Recruiters and hiring managers will often ask these staff members about their opinion of candidates based on their initial interaction and engagement. Also, if you do land the job, you want to ensure that your first encounter with your future colleagues was a pleasant one.

Behavior-based Interview Technique

Candidates should familiarize themselves with the behavior-based interview technique, also referred to as the "S.T.A.R." technique. Most companies have adopted this type of interviewing to determine if past behaviors will determine future performance.

S	Situation	What was the situation?
T	Task	What was required?
A	Action	What did you do and why?
R	Result	What was the outcome?

You will know if you are being asked a S.T.A.R. based interview question if the question starts off with *"Tell me about a time..."* or *"Give me an example of...."* Pick the right story, make a solid statement and finish strong. There are several behavior-based interview preparation websites and Apps (too many to list here) where you can practice questions and answers to help prepare you for an actual interview.

Situational-based Interview Technique

Another popular interview technique is situational-based questions. These generally start off with *"What would you do if..."* or *"How would you handle..."*, and requires the candidate to provide feedback on how they would react when faced with a hypothetical work-related situation. These scenarios may be based on an actual business situation the candidate may face once employed for the company. This line of interview questioning also allows the candidate to demonstrate their problem solving and analytical skills, as well as how well they think on their feet with little preparation.

Also, be sure to ask relevant and targeted questions as it relates to the company and the position. This is your opportunity to interview THEM! Ask why the position is open (vacancy or new position?). If it is a vacancy, what happened to the predecessor (promoted or left the organization?). How is the company performing financially? What are the goals of the organization and the department, and how well are they tracking towards achieving them? What is the company and departmental culture? Do team members go to lunch or happy hour together? It is also acceptable to ask if there is anything about your experience or background that would cause them concern about hiring you for the position. Do you have gaps in your experience, or are you "over-qualified"? Keep these questions in your interview toolkit and ask each of them during your interviews to ensure you know if this position is truly a fit for you and for them.

Finally, it is perfectly fine to ask the recruiter or interviewer where they are in the hiring process. Most interviewers will be comfortable letting candidates know if they are in the beginning phase and just starting to bring people in for interviews, or if they are starting to wrap up interviews and plan on making a decision soon. This will help you gauge how long it may take before you hear back from the interviewer.

Interview Worksheet

S	Situation	What was the situation?
T	Task	What was required?
A	Action	What did you do and why?
R	Result	What was the outcome?

Situation	
Task	
Action	
Result	

Situation	
Task	
Action	
Result	

Situation	
Task	
Action	
Result	

Situation	
Task	
Action	
Result	

TIP 5 - Proper Follow-Up After Your Interview

The art of thank you notes is NOT dead. Depending on the recruiter or hiring manager, candidates could potentially eliminate themselves from consideration for a position by NOT sending a formal follow-up thank you note. The recommendation is to err on the side of caution and send one after each interview – phone and in person – either the same day or within 24 hours. This is your final opportunity to leave a lasting and positive impression on the interviewer. If you interviewed with multiple people at the same company, be certain to customize sections of your thank you note by including key points you discussed with each interviewer. If a panel interviewed you, then send one follow-up note to the group. Be certain to collect business cards or contact information from each person who interviewed you that day. Do not **ever** send any of your follow-up communication by text message. This is not only inappropriate, but may go against the culture of the organization…and can make you appear a bit like a stalker! An email or handwritten thank you notes are still the only acceptable written forms of follow-up communication.

Your thank you note should be two to three paragraphs at the most. Use this final form of contact to reiterate the key points discussed during your interview, inclusive of what their needs are and how your particular experience, knowledge, skills and abilities will meet those needs and help solve their problems. Remember, the job description is the company's "cry for help" and a great resource to pull key phrases and responsibilities, then weave them throughout your follow-up communication.

Remember, these days, most companies are taking, on average, 45 to 90 days to fill open positions; therefore, you may not hear back from the recruiter or hiring manager immediately. After you send your follow-up note, give the interviewer a call after two or three weeks to find out where they are in the hiring process. As mentioned in **TIP 4**, you should also ask this question during your in-person interview.

If, after two or three weeks, you have not heard back from the interviewer, wait another two weeks and send another brief follow-up note letting them know you are still interested in the position and why you know you are the right fit for the role. After four to six weeks, make one final call to the recruiter or interviewer, again expressing your continued interest in the position and your strong desire to join their team. The best times to call are **before** 9:00 am and **after** 5:00 pm, when most people are just starting their day or ending it. In most cases you will contact the recruiter or hiring manager directly, since their assistant may not be screening their calls outside of those core business hours. Even if you do not land that particular position, you will have made a lasting and positive impression on the interviewer and they may keep you in mind for future opportunities.

TIP 6 - Tips for the 50+ Year-Old Candidate

This century represents the first time some companies are experiencing four to five generations in the workplace. What it takes to motivate each generation is distinctly different, and the good companies are tuned into both the necessary extrinsic and intrinsic motivators, and are adjusting their business practices accordingly, (i.e., performance management, benefit offerings, hiring and promotion practices).

Looking for a new job over the age of 50 can prove challenging, but it is important to keep things in perspective. There are several companies that welcome the experience of *"seasoned"* professionals and understand the security and loyalty they bring to the job. However, there are companies opting for more millennials to fill newly created positions or those vacated by retirees. Millennials are deemed to be quick learners, *"digital natives"*, eager and cheaper to hire. However, there is a cost companies are paying for hiring the millennials – turnover! It costs companies significant money to both hire and lose employees. Research shows millennials tend to remain with an employer on average one-and-a-half to two years, at which point they start to feel it is time for them to move on in order to gain new experiences, or a promotion that their current company may not feel they are quite ready for. This can be the hidden sweet spot for the 50+ year-old candidate. Your experience working across multiple generations in the workplace is a true value and shows how you excel at adapting to changing environments.

During the application and hiring practices, be certain to express how your years of experience can add value to the organization. It is also important to look for ways to build your social media brand (i.e., LinkedIn© profile) and improve your use of office technology. Seek help from a professional Career Coach or organization if this is a challenging area for you. Be certain to read **TIP 12 – *The Importance of Your Personal Brand***, for more details on personal branding and using social media in your job search.

Also, do not underestimate the value of updating your wardrobe. If you have not added new pieces to your closet in five or more years, it is time to go shopping! Think of someone whose style you admire. Hire an image consultant, or recruit a close friend or family member who will be open and honest with you about how to update your look. Updating your image should also include your hairstyle/haircut, makeup and accessories.

Finally, please be certain to stay on top of your industry! Information and technology are changing at a rapid pace. Stay informed by reading industry-specific magazines or newsletters, attend seminars and workshops or continuing education courses to help keep your knowledge and skill set relevant. When updating your resume, consider consolidating experience that is beyond 15 – 20 years old. You may also want to consider removing graduation dates from your resume if you graduated more than 20 years ago. Instead, just list the school and degree obtained. That is the only information that should be relevant to your future employer.

Some alternative career paths for the seasoned 50+ year-old professionals include part-time work, temporary assignments, consulting, volunteering, and entrepreneurship. Each of these options will help you build upon past business experience and skills, keep you relevant in the job market, and expand your professional network. All of these are keys to a successful transition at this pivotal point in your career.

[5]Motivating Five Generations in the Workplace

Traditionalists

Traditionalists are motivated by money, but also want to be respected.

Preferred recognition style: subtle, personalized recognition and feedback.
Welcomed benefits: long-term care insurance, catch-up retirement funding.

Baby Boomers

Baby Boomers prefer monetary rewards, but also value flexible retirement planning and peer recognition.

Preferred recognition style: acknowledgement of their input and expertise; prestigious job titles, parking places and office size are measures of success.
Welcomed benefits: 401(k) matching funds, sabbaticals, catch-up retirement funding.

Generation X

Generation X values bonuses and stock as monetary rewards and workplace flexibility as a non-monetary reward.

Preferred recognition style: informal, rapid and publicly communicated.
Welcomed benefits: telecommuting and tuition reimbursement.

Generation Y

Generation Y wants stock options as a monetary reward and values feedback as a non-monetary reward.

Preferred recognition style: regular, informal communication through company chat or social networks.
Welcomed benefits: flexible schedules, continued learning.

Generation Z

Generation Z is more interested in social rewards (mentorship and constant feedback) than money, but also is motivated by meaningful work and being given responsibility.

Preferred recognition style: regular in-person public praise.
Welcomed benefits: online training and certification programs.

TIP 7 – Negotiation and Acceptance

Know your worth, and always, always, always negotiate the **JOB**, not the **SALARY**. Focus on how your experience can help move the company forward and achieve their goals. This approach emphasizes how your contribution will bring value to the organization. There are several websites dedicated to educating candidates about salary ranges in their geographies, or geographies where the job is located (**see APPENDIX**). These sites take into consideration your years of experience, education level, specialized certifications or licenses, as well as the size and industry of the company. Total Rewards are also a factor when considering the salary package. If you cannot negotiate the base salary, you can often negotiate other components of the Total Rewards package.

Sample of a Total Rewards Package:

- Base Salary
- 401(k) Match
- Deferred Compensation
- Transportation

- Paid Time Off & Holidays
- Relocation Package
- Sign-on Bonus

- Bonuses/Increases
- Profit Sharing
- Stock Options

- Education Reimbursement
- Other Perks (free/subsidized meals/beverages; free parking)

By negotiating the **JOB**, you are able to distinguish how your particular experience may go above and beyond what is required based on the job description. Use this conversation as an opportunity to not only express why are you interested in the position, regardless of the salary, but also how you will close any gaps that perhaps the company has not even considered as it relates to the position. Negotiating the salary is being shortsighted. Generally, companies have established salary ranges, and look to hire close to the mid-point or higher, depending on the local market and competition to fill certain positions, at which time the company may hire as high as the 75th percentile within those established salary ranges.

Another key negotiation method is to accept the position, but negotiate to have your performance reviewed in three or six months, with a salary adjustment on par with your original desired salary. This gives you the opportunity to show how well you can perform in the role, and lets the employer see what they are getting for the money. If there is a position at the next level, review that job description and do your best to consistently operate at the next level. This gives you more negotiation power.

Do not accept the first offer unless it is truly where you want to be. Remember, going into a new company and new position are the only opportunities where you may successfully negotiate an increase of 15 - 20 percent or more over and above your current salary. Once you accept the offer and are employed by the company, you can expect to receive incremental salary increases ranging from 2 percent to 5 percent, if you are lucky! Other than these merit increases, the only other opportunity to gain a significant bump up in pay while employed with the same employer will be through internal promotions, where you may gain up to a double-digit increase to bring you to the mid-salary range at the next level.

At some point during the job search, candidates may be faced with a recruiter who may ask about their current or most recent salary, or request submission of paystubs or tax returns to validate their current salary. Some states have passed laws making these types of questions illegal on job applications and during the interview process (i.e., New York and Massachusetts). Providing this information before you have an offer will put you on the defense and at a huge disadvantage. You will also relinquish your negotiating power. This is particularly the case for female job applicants, who are still currently paid below their male counterparts for the same position. Consider the fact that a contractor will not tell you what their last client paid them, so why should you share something as intimate as your current or most recent salary with a total stranger? Now the recruiter is basing your value primarily on your most recent salary. This can be concerning, especially if you were underpaid, which may occur again in the new company if you share your historical salary information. Also, do not include your salary history in your cover letter or resume, even if requested.

An alternative way to respond to the dreaded question, *"How much are you currently making?"*; or *"What was your last salary?"*; or *"Please provide your salary history"*, is to simply respond with: *"I am currently focused on administrative assistant positions in the $60,000 to $65,000 range. Does this position fit within that range?"* Now you are speaking their language…salary ranges! You also present yourself as professional and knowledgeable about your value in the marketplace. There is no need to provide your actual salary information when you respond in this manner. Recruiters may ask this question upfront to determine if your salary expectations are within their salary ranges. This helps avoid wasting their time and yours, so feel free to use the above statement, whether you are asked this question at the front end of the interview process or at the end of the process.

Finally, take time to pause before responding to or accepting an offer. Ask to have a day to consider the offer. This will give you time to do more salary research, especially now that you have the verbal offer in hand. Talk the offer over with friends or family during this time and make certain you are comfortable going back to the negotiation table. Refer to the **Appendix** for a listing of valuable salary data resources. Just remember, negotiation is expected. NEVER leave money on the table!

TIP 8 – The First 90 Days

Goals! Goals! Goals! This needs to be your singular focus when you start a new job or position. In the same way the President of the United States has a 100-day plan, we should manage our new job or new position/promotion in the same manner. Work with your direct manager to establish your goals for the first 90 days. Focus on three to four goals each month and meet monthly to measure your progress along the way. Monthly check-ins will allow you time to reset goals in case the needs of the business or your manager have changed during the course of that particular month. Establishing these goals and having monthly check-ins will also help manage expectations...both yours and those of your manager, team members and other stakeholders who may be affected by your progress. Today's organizations are often made up of matrix reporting structures, meaning you may report to or work with multiple "managers" and teams. It is important to understand these complex relationships early in your new role and understand your value across each of these stakeholder groups.

Next, look for the low hanging fruit. Are there immediate changes you can implement that will help move the company forward? Are there immediate improvements you can make in your position or through improving efficiencies that will positively demonstrate your value to the organization? Look for these opportunities early on, and communicate with your manager and other key stakeholders who can be champions for you and support you as you implement these changes or improvements, and who can help you avoid any known or unknown company landmines, (i.e., those who may not be fans of "change").

Be certain to spend time establishing your internal network. Go to lunch, breakfast or coffee, or schedule 15 to 30 minute meetings with key people across the organization during your first 90 days on the job. Get to know their pain points, and understand what "good" looks like to them. Gain a sense of how you can positively impact their work life and make their job easier. Remember, you were brought on to the team to fill a void and to answer the company's "cry for help", so make the investment spending time with those who will benefit from you joining the team and the organization at large. Take lots of notes and follow up after your meetings with a recap of your key takeaways and next steps, along with anticipated timing or due dates.

Finally, pace yourself! Do not over-commit and under-deliver, but rather under-commit and over-deliver. People will remember how you made them feel. You want to be known as the person who is true to their word and someone who follows through and completes high quality tasks efficiently, effectively and timely. You are establishing your reputation and your brand with each interaction within those first 90 days (see more Personal Branding details in **TIP 11**). Use your time wisely and take time to celebrate your wins!

TIP 9 - Who's in Your Front Row?

Some organizations have a Board of Directors. You should treat your career in the same manner. Establish a core group of supporters in your *front row* who will be honest and candid with you, and provide ongoing guidance and feedback as you grow your career. Anyone who is not part of this core support group belongs in the back row or balcony of your life, and should have little, if any, influence on your career goals. The members of your front row should always be willing to tell you when you are right and when you are wrong. They are not supposed to be "yes" people, but rather a group of trusted advisors. Below is a description of each of the key members of your personal Board of Directors.

Secure a **Mentor** in your life. The role of the Mentor is to provide a safe zone and help you with establishing goals, action steps and key milestones to help move your career forward. Mentoring is a long-term relationship. This person serves as your advisor, confidant and moral supporter, all while helping to keep you motivated and grounded throughout your career. The Mentor's role is to provide guidance to help you develop for both current and future positions throughout your career. Preferably, Mentors should not be employed at your current company, and may or may not be in your same industry or field of expertise. Your Mentor should be someone you view as a role model based on their own personal and professional achievements. Your Mentor will stay with you throughout your career, and help guide you as you grow professionally from one position or company to the next. Mentors are current-based, meaning they are consistently working with you where you are now, and giving you the tools to move you to the next level or expand your current position.

You should also secure a **Sponsor** or **Advocate** at your current company. This should be someone who will serve as your personal supporter, who will promote you and your skills with key decision-makers. The Sponsor/Advocate will open doors for you at your company, and ensure you are connected with the right people and get assigned to the right teams or projects that will give you the exposure you need to move your career forward. Sponsors/Advocates vouch for you in the inner circles of the company, and will recommend you for key assignments that will put you in front of the people who can grow your career within that company. Sponsors/Advocates are future-based, meaning they are there to help you get to a future position, team or project within the company.

Everyone should have a **Coach** at some point in his or her career. Today's organizations are moving fast and constantly changing. At some point, everyone will struggle with adjusting to change, and adapting their skill set to help them remain a viable and nimble team member. Although the relationship with a Coach is short-term and task-oriented, it can benefit you in many ways. A Coach will spend time getting to know you and your primary goal(s), and partner with you as you develop action steps to achieve the goal you have set for yourself. A Coach's role is not to TELL you what to do, as most times you already know what needs to be done, but just need a dedicated partner to help keep you focused and hold you accountable to yourself. The Coach may partner with you on personal (i.e., work/life balance) or professional goals (i.e., transitioning from a transactional to a strategic thinker).

Depending on the type of engagement, a Coach may also meet with your immediate manager, direct reports or other team members to gain a 360-view of your core strengths and areas for development to focus on during the coaching engagement. Some organizations hire Coaches to help new or young managers, or to help an employee develop or strengthen a particular competency (i.e., managing more effectively). Working with a Coach used to be viewed as an organization's last attempt to develop an employee before terminating them for underperforming. However, companies have transitioned over the years to embrace coaching as a perk and an additional benefit for their high performers and employees in their succession plan. Sometimes the company will pay for coaching services, while other times the employee will pay for coaching. Either way, coaching is now accepted as a necessary investment at some point in your career.

If you are transitioning to a new team, department or company, seek out the local *Advisor/Interpreter*. This is the individual who can share the company and team history with you. Their purpose is to help you avoid "landmines" and to help you understand and interpret the people politics and team dynamics of the group you are joining.

Each of these partnerships will be key to help you navigate your career and your new position. Seek those who you can trust and who have your best interest at heart. These relationships should happen organically and naturally, and feel authentic. There will be times when you will have each of these "seats" filled, and other times when you may only have a couple or a few of them filled, and that is perfectly fine. Knowing who you need to have in your front row at any given time is all about where you are in your career and what gaps you have in our personal and professional development areas.

Your Board of Directors

Mentor Candidates:	
Sponsor/Advocate Candidates:	
Career Coach Candidates:	
Advisor/Interpreter Candidates:	

TIP 10 - Promote, Transfer or Transition: The Choice is Yours!

Promotion

When you are seeking a promotion at your current employer, you have to think of the process in the same manner as politicians who are running for office. You need to attract constituents. Be visible and take the lead on key projects and assignments. You need to gain key supporters and decision-makers. You need to have some champions and some cheerleaders out in front of you. You need to have a good support team around you. You need to have a good Mentor and a good Sponsor/Advocate who will provide you with feedback and guidance along the way. Seeking a promotion is an exercise in strategy, and will take careful planning along the way.

You should also have ongoing conversations with your direct manager to let him or her know what your career goals are so they can help get you there. Remember, they cannot read your mind, so if you do not tell them that you are seeking a promotion at some point in your career, they may not automatically think it is of interest to you. Finally, toot your own horn. Keep track of your success and contributions to the organization. Be prepared to share how you improved efficiencies, generated revenue or saved the company money.

Most importantly...be your own advocate!

Transfer

Transferring to a different department or team is another great way to grow your skill set and your career. Whether the transfer is a lateral move or a promotion, do not underestimate the value of being a part of a new team, department or project. Transfers allow you to learn about new and different parts of your organization, and will help build your internal network, especially if you have been with the same team for a long period of time. Transferring will help get you out of your comfort zone, while expanding skills you have already gained. Skills are like muscles...the more you use them, the stronger they get! Some companies also offer *stretch assignments*, where employees are loaned out for a short period of time (i.e., six months or less) to other divisions to help with project deadlines, or lend their particular area of expertise to complete a particular task. This may or may not come with a salary increase or title change, but do not let that hold you back if presented with this opportunity. Consider this an additional opportunity for personal and professional development, and a chance to help define what you do and do not want in your next career move. Use it to your advantage!

Internal Interviewing

When you go in for an interview, it is always a good opportunity to take a look around and get a sense of what the culture is like for that particular company. Well, the same principle applies if you are looking for an internal position. You must understand what that particular department's culture is like, what the team's culture is like, and what type of culture the manager is cultivating within that team. This assessment will help you truly know whether or not joining that team will be a good fit for you and your career goals. If you are approached with an opportunity for a promotion, but you know long-term the position or team will not be a good fit for you or your goals, you should diplomatically turn down the opportunity. Some people may be concerned that this could ruin their chances for future promotional opportunities, when it fact it is demonstrating a high level of professionalism and maturity. It is important to know that every opportunity is not for you. You want to work within your strengths, and do not want to take on an opportunity where you may potentially fail or not perform at your best. Do your research, just as you would for an external position. Know when to say YES and when to say NO!

Transition

If you have sought a promotion or a transfer and neither has come to fruition, and you feel it will not happen at your current company, then it is time to consider a transition (i.e., exit strategy). Using **TIPS 1 – 9** will help guide you through the transition process and help you establish a solid plan of action to help you land the right job at the right company.

TIP 11 - The Importance of Your Personal Brand

Your Brand is...
- your calling card.
- what you are known for.
- how people experience you.
- about bringing who you ARE to what you DO...and how you DO IT.

In other words, your personal brand is how you show up!

Your personal brand is the *sweet spot* between how you see yourself and how others view you. It is extremely important to protect your personal brand in the same manner that companies do for their brand. Consider yourself the product and you are in charge of marketing that product each and every day, verbally, in writing and visually. You have put a lot of time, work, dedication, education and development into this product called Y-O-U, and you should want to protect your product and make certain it is always presented in the best possible light.

It takes only seven (7) seconds to make a first impression. This is an important factor to consider when you are meeting with and interacting with others. Be approachable and accessible. What impression do you want them to walk away with after meeting you for the first time? People may not always remember what you said, but they will remember how you made them feel. These are all factors to consider as you look to develop and refine your personal brand.

Take responsibility for your actions and hold yourself accountable, even if no one is around to witness it. This will go a long way in building your personal brand. If you make a mistake, own up to it, accept the consequences, identify the lessons learned and move on. Do not try to cover it up or lie about it. Someone once said that it takes years to build a reputation (e.g., personal brand) and only seconds to ruin it. Lying will ruin your reputation in seconds!

People want to work with people they feel they know and like. Be intentional. Be authentic. Be yourself!

"You're never wrong to do the right thing" – Mark Twain

Social Media and Personal Branding

A Google© search will likely list all of your social media profiles, even if your accounts are private. You should keep your personal social media pages private to ensure no content is accessible to employers (i.e., photos, posts, blogs, etc.). This should include personal accounts on Facebook©, Instagram©, Periscope©, Snapchat©, Pinterest©, personal blogs, etc. You can also use your settings on Facebook© to ensure your profile does not appear in Google© searches.

Although it is illegal for employers to discriminate against candidates based solely on the information obtained from social media accounts, it is advisable to keep your personal accounts private to ensure there is less information available to cause a potential employer any concerns about hiring you. This may include political or religious views, comments about current or former employers/managers, or certain social activities that may not fit the culture of a future employer.

Currently, LinkedIn© is the professional social media website most used by companies, recruiters and hiring managers to research candidates. Keep your profile up to date, include a targeted headline and summary, upload a professional headshot, and join relevant industry, school alumni, and professional organization groups. Also, be certain to include relevant skills and seek endorsements from peers and others in your network. You should also ask for recommendations from current or former co-workers, clients or managers for each of the positions you list on your profile. All of this information will help build out your profile and make it more appealing to recruiters and hiring managers.

Your LinkedIn© profile provides more information about you than you can cover on your resume. Although some people like to do so, there is no real need to upload your resume to your LinkedIn© profile. Your profile can be downloaded and saved as a PDF document. Plus, you want to give the recruiter a reason to contact you. If you attach your full resume to your profile, the recruiter can decide you are not a viable candidate before having the opportunity to speak with you. Make them want to connect with you to find out more about you. Use your profile as the *carrot* to reel them in, THEN make your pitch and deliver your "wow factor" when you have your initial conversation. If the recruiter determines you are not a good fit for the position, offer to refer someone to them who may be a better fit. This will go a long way in building your brand with the recruiter, and they will keep you in mind for future opportunities.

The Elevator Pitch

Every professional should establish a good elevator pitch and revise it as you grow your career. Your pitch should be 30-60 seconds in length and briefly explain the following:
- Who are you?
- How have you made an impact?
- What sets you apart from the competition?
- What are you seeking?
- Why are you a good fit for the company/position?

Practice your elevator pitch in the mirror; record it and listen to it, paying close attention to how concise and succinct you are in your delivery; practice it in your head as you ride on an elevator; and, use it with friends and family and ask for their feedback. Once perfected, your elevator pitch should be used when you introduce yourself at networking events, when you meet new business contacts at professional conferences and seminars, and any other opportunity where you can leave an impression, exchange contact information, and follow up for future career opportunities. As you grow and develop in your career, and add new skills and accomplishments, your elevator pitch should adjust accordingly. Refresh it every year to remain current and relevant within your targeted industry.

Job hunting and growing your career will take focus, a targeted strategy, and most importantly: a solid **Pace, Persistence, Perseverance** and lots of **Patience**! Good luck in your endeavors!

Your Elevator Pitch

Who are you?	
How have you made an impact?	
What sets you apart from the competition?	
What are you seeking?	
Why are you a good fit for the company/position?	

APPENDIX

REFERENCES

[1,3] The Five O'clock Club

[2] Top 10 Resume Fonts: Monster.com
(http://www.monster.com/career-advice/article/best-font-for-resume)

[4] www.thesororitysecrets.com

[5] Society for Human Resources Management (SHRM), May 2016

JOB SEARCH RESOURCES

The list below is updated as of the date of publication. Due to constantly changing technology and resources, the list may require annual updating.

www.Linkedin.com (*company job listings; direct contacts; networking*)

www.Indeed.com (*aggregate job board*)

www.Simplyhired.com (*aggregate job board*)

www.Linkup.com (*aggregate job board*)

www.Idealist.org (*non-profit job listings*)

www.USAjobs.gov (*government job listings*)

www.Upwork.com
(*freelancers' database and project listings*)

www.Freelanship.com
(*freelancers' database and project listings*)

www.Dice.com (*technology job listings*)

www.Crunchboard.com
(*official job board of TechCrunch; technology job listings*)

www.Elevatedcareers.com
(*job matchmaker; an eHarmony© company*)

www.Twellow.com
(*locate industry-specific Twitter connections; networking*)

www.Jibberjobber.com
(*digital job hunting and networking tracker*)

Various Professional and Alumni Organizations

SALARY DATA RESOURCES

Google

<u>KEY INDUSTRY RESOURCES</u>

Google

USEFUL JOB HUNTING APPS

The list below is updated as of the date of publication. Due to constantly changing technology and resources, the list may require annual updating.

- **Charlie Personal Assistant**
  (*App that syncs with your calendar and locates information/articles on the internet for people with whom you have meetings scheduled. Must include their full name in your calendar invite/reminder.*)

- **Job Interview Question & Answer**
  (*App lists several typical behavior-based and situational-based job interview questions for all levels, along with examples of how to respond.*)

- **Mock Job Interview App – Question & Answer**
  (*App provides video recorded questions for typical behavior-based and situational-based job interview questions for all levels. You can practice and record your answer, and review it prior to conducting formal phone or in-person interviews.*)

- **Switch Job Matching**
  (*App aggregates jobs based on your defined search criteria and allows you to apply directly, chat with the recruiter/hiring manager, or share with your network. You can share your profile or remain anonymous.*)

- **Samcard Professional Business Card Reader**
  (*App allows you to scan business cards and upload directly to your phone's contact list. No need to keep business cards!*)

Also check out www.theinterviewguys.com as a great additional resource for interview questions and answers!

CONTACT INFO:

Tana M. Session
Speaker/Coach/Trainer/Consultant
www.tanamsession.com
tana@tanamsession.com

LinkedIn: @Tana M. Session
Twitter: @tanatane
Instagram: @tanamsession
Facebook: @TMS Tana M Session

87839031R00044